BULL RUN 2024

Your Guide to Mastering
the Next Bullish Market

FREDERICK STRONG

Bull Run 2024

Copyright © 2024 by Frederick Strong

All rights reserved. No part of this publication may be reproduced, distributed, or transmitted in any form or by any means, including photocopying, recording, or other electronic or mechanical methods, without the prior written permission of the publisher, except in the case of brief quotations embodied in critical reviews and certain other noncommercial uses permitted by copyright law.

Contents

Introduction 1
    A Brief History of Bull Runs in the Crypto Space 3
    2024: The Unique Confluence of Factors 7
    Who This Book is For 9

Chapter 1 13
The Cryptocurrency Ecosystem 13
    Blockchain Technology 16
    Major Cryptocurrencies 20
    Market Cycles 22

Chapter 2 25
Bull Market Mechanics 25
    What Drives Bull Runs? 25
    Identifying Early Signs of a Bull Market 29
    Basic Technical Analysis for Interpreting Charts. 30

Chapter 3 41
Risk and Reward 41
    Investing vs. Trading: 44
    Risk Management 48
    Setting Realistic Goals and Managing Expectations 52

Chapter 4 55
Market Analysis 55
    What's Happened Since the Last Bull Run? ... 55
    2024 Predictions: What the Experts Are Saying. 57
    Potential Catalysts and Roadblocks 59

Chapter 5.. 63
Investment Strategies..63

    Assessing Risk Tolerance and Financial
    Objectives.. 64
    Spot Trading vs. Derivatives........................... 67
    Building a Diversified Crypto Portfolio.............68

Chapter 6... 73
Emerging Trends... 73

    DeFi..73
    NFTs.. 76
    The Metaverse.. 78
    Telegram Based Play-to-Earn earn Games and
    Their Tokens...80
        Hamster Kombat...................................... 82
        MemeFi... 86
        TapSwap... 90
        My Thoughts on Telegram Based
        Play-to-Earn Games.................................94

Chapter 7... 97
Choosing the Right Exchange.............................97

    Centralized vs. Decentralized Exchanges
    (CEXs vs. DEXs)...98
    Going through KYC... 103
    Comparing Popular Exchanges.................... 104

Chapter 8... 109
Wallet Security... 109

    Hot Wallets vs. Cold Wallets......................... 110
    Safeguarding Your Private Keys................... 115

Chapter 9..119
Staying Informed..119

Reliable News Sources................................. 122
Social Media Handles to Follow..................... 123
Online Communities....................................... 124
Identifying and Avoiding Scams, FUD, and Misinformation..126

Chapter 10... 129
The Emotional Rollercoaster............................ 129
The Psychology of Investing......................... 130
Strategies for Emotional Mastery.................. 131

Conclusion... 133
Glossary of Crypto Terms................................. 135
About the Author.. 141

Bull Run 2024

Introduction

A bull run in crypto refers to a sustained period of rising prices across the cryptocurrency market. During a bull run, investor confidence typically increases, leading to higher trading volumes and overall positive sentiment. This can result in significant price increases for various cryptocurrencies over a relatively short period. This, my friends, is the exhilarating phenomenon known as a bull run – a period of sustained upward momentum in the cryptocurrency market. It's a time when fortunes are made, dreams are realized, and the future seems boundless.

The adrenaline rush of a bull run is like nothing else. It's the thrill of watching your investments multiply in value, seemingly overnight. It's the satisfaction of seeing your careful research and calculated risks pay off. But beyond the financial gains, a bull run is a transformative experience. It can empower individuals, uplift communities, and even reshape entire industries.

Bull Run 2024

I know the success story of Vanessa, a young American professional who invested a modest sum in Bitcoin during the 2017 bull run. As Bitcoin's price skyrocketed to a peak of nearly $19,188, Vanessa's investment grew exponentially. She was able to pay off her student loans, invest in her dream startup, and even purchase her first home. Vanessa's story is not unique; countless individuals across the United States and the world have experienced life-changing financial gains through crypto bull runs.

But a bull run isn't just about individual success stories; it has a ripple effect throughout the market. As prices climb, more investors are drawn in, fueling further growth. This increased demand attracts media attention, sparking conversations about the potential of cryptocurrencies to revolutionize finance and technology. It's a time when innovation flourishes, new projects emerge, and the entire ecosystem thrives.

In 2020, Bitcoin surged from around $7,161 at the beginning of the year to close at an impressive $28,993. Ethereum, not to be outdone, saw an even more meteoric rise, starting the year around $130 and closing at roughly $737. The impact of this bull run was felt across the United States, as more people began to understand and embrace the potential of cryptocurrencies. It paved the way for increased adoption, wider acceptance, and a thriving crypto community in the country.

As we look ahead to 2024, the anticipation for another bull run is palpable. The confluence of factors, including the Bitcoin halving and growing institutional interest, suggests that we may be on the cusp of another exhilarating chapter in the crypto story. Are you ready to be part of it?

A Brief History of Bull Runs in the Crypto Space

The cryptocurrency market, much like a roller coaster, has experienced dramatic highs and lows throughout its relatively short history. Each bull run, a period of sustained upward price movement, has been unique, driven by a distinct set of factors and leaving its mark on the evolving landscape of digital assets.

2010-2011: The Early Adopters' Bull Run

Bitcoin, the pioneer of cryptocurrencies, saw its first significant price surge in 2010-2011. This initial bull run was fueled primarily by early adopters and tech enthusiasts who recognized the potential of Bitcoin's decentralized and borderless nature. Bitcoin's price jumped from $0.10 in October 2010 to a peak of $29.60 in June 2011. This early rally, though short-lived, laid the groundwork for Bitcoin's future growth and established it as a legitimate asset class.

2013: Bitcoin Breaks Through

The 2013 bull run marked a turning point for Bitcoin as it crossed the $1,000 threshold for the first time. Increased media attention, growing merchant adoption, and the emergence of cryptocurrency exchanges all contributed to this surge. The price of Bitcoin started the year at $13 and reached an astonishing $1,151 by December, a staggering increase of over 8,700%. This bull run cemented Bitcoin's position as the leading cryptocurrency and sparked global interest in the potential of digital assets.

2017: The ICO Boom and Mainstream Mania

The 2017 bull run was a watershed moment for the entire crypto market, fueled by the explosion of Initial Coin Offerings (ICOs) and a surge of mainstream attention. Bitcoin's price surged from around $968 at the beginning of the year to an all-time high of nearly $20,000 in December. This unprecedented rally was accompanied by a proliferation of new cryptocurrencies and blockchain projects, attracting both seasoned investors and newcomers alike. While the ICO boom ultimately led to a market correction, it also laid the foundation for a more diverse and mature crypto ecosystem.

2020-2021: Institutional Adoption and DeFi Revolution

The most recent bull run, spanning 2020-2021, was characterized by increased institutional adoption and the rise of decentralized finance (DeFi). Major financial institutions like PayPal and Square began offering crypto services, while companies like MicroStrategy and Tesla added Bitcoin to their balance sheets. Bitcoin's price surged from around $7,200 in January 2020 to an all-time high of $64,895 in April 2021. Ethereum also experienced a dramatic rise, driven by the growing popularity of DeFi applications and the anticipation of the Ethereum 2.0 upgrade. This bull run demonstrated the increasing maturity of the crypto market and its potential to disrupt traditional finance.

The Evolving Landscape

Each bull run has brought new developments and challenges to the crypto market. From the early days of Bitcoin's niche appeal to the current landscape of institutional investment and decentralized finance, the market has matured significantly. The 2024 bull run, if it materializes, is expected to be driven by a new set of factors, including the growing adoption of cryptocurrencies in emerging markets like Africa and Australia, the integration of blockchain technology into traditional industries, and the increasing demand for digital assets as a hedge against inflation.

2024: The Unique Confluence of Factors

2024 is shaping up to be a pivotal year in the cryptocurrency world, with several key factors converging to create a potential breeding ground for a bull run. Let's break down these elements:

The Bitcoin Halving:

- **Simple:** Every four years, the rate at which new Bitcoins are created is cut in half. This event, known as the "halving," reduces the available supply of Bitcoin, potentially leading to a price increase if demand remains steady or grows. Think of it like a rare item becoming even rarer – its value naturally goes up.
- **Deeper:** The halving has historically been a catalyst for bull runs, as it creates a supply shock that can trigger a significant shift in the supply-demand balance. For seasoned investors, the halving presents an opportunity to accumulate Bitcoin before the potential price increase. Additionally,

the halving's impact on miner profitability and network security can offer valuable insights for those looking to understand the underlying dynamics of the Bitcoin ecosystem.

Increased Institutional Adoption: The Big Players Enter the Game

- **Simple:** Major financial institutions and corporations are increasingly recognizing the value of cryptocurrencies. They're investing in Bitcoin and other digital assets, integrating crypto into their services, and even building their own blockchain infrastructure. This influx of institutional money is a strong indicator of growing confidence in the crypto market.
- **Deeper:** Institutional adoption not only brings significant capital into the market but also lends credibility to cryptocurrencies as a legitimate asset class. For seasoned investors, this trend can signal a shift in the overall market sentiment and open up new opportunities for strategic investments. It's

also worth noting that institutional involvement can lead to the development of new financial products and services, further expanding the crypto market's reach.

Who This Book is For

Whether you're a curious newcomer or a seasoned crypto veteran, this book is your compass for navigating the thrilling and potentially lucrative landscape of the 2024 bull run.

For Beginners:

If you're just starting your crypto journey, this book will be your trusted guide. We'll break down the complex world of cryptocurrencies into easily digestible chunks, explaining the fundamental concepts in plain English. You'll learn:

- **The Basics:** What is blockchain? How do crypto wallets work? Which exchanges are best for Nigerian investors? We'll answer these questions and more, laying a solid foundation for your crypto education.

- **Bull Run 101:** We'll demystify the mechanics of bull markets, explaining what drives them and how to spot the early signs. You'll learn how to read charts, interpret indicators, and understand the psychology of market cycles.
- **Getting Started:** We'll guide you through the process of buying, storing, and managing your crypto investments. You'll learn how to choose the right wallet, protect your assets, and avoid common pitfalls.

By the end of this book, you'll have the knowledge and confidence to make informed decisions in the exciting world of cryptocurrencies.

For Experienced Investors:

If you're already familiar with the crypto market, this book will be your strategic edge. We'll delve into advanced concepts and strategies tailored to the unique dynamics of the 2024 bull run. You'll gain insights into:

- **Market Analysis:** We'll dissect the current market landscape, providing expert opinions, forecasts, and in-depth analysis of potential catalysts and roadblocks.

- **Investment Strategies:** We'll explore advanced portfolio building techniques, diversification strategies, and the pros and cons of various investment approaches, including spot trading, derivatives, and DeFi.

- **Emerging Trends:** We'll look into the latest developments in decentralized finance (DeFi), non-fungible tokens (NFTs), and the metaverse, highlighting potential investment opportunities and risks.

By the end of this book, you'll be equipped with the tools and strategies you need to maximize your gains and minimize your risks in the 2024 bull run.

No matter where you are on your crypto journey, this book is designed to empower you with the knowledge, insights, and strategies you need to thrive in the exciting world of cryptocurrencies. Whether you're aiming for financial freedom, looking to diversify your portfolio, or simply fascinated by this groundbreaking technology, we'll guide you every step of the way.

Chapter 1

The Cryptocurrency Ecosystem

In the past decade, the world has witnessed a financial revolution brought about by the rise of cryptocurrency. What started as an obscure technology experiment has evolved into a global phenomenon that has reshaped how we perceive and interact with money. Cryptocurrencies are digital or virtual currencies that use cryptography for security, making them difficult to counterfeit or double-spend. The most well-known cryptocurrency, Bitcoin, was created in 2009 by an anonymous person or group of people using the pseudonym Satoshi Nakamoto. Since then, thousands of alternative cryptocurrencies have been developed, each with unique features and applications.

The journey of cryptocurrency from its inception to mainstream acceptance is a fascinating tale of innovation, resilience, and disruption. In its early days, Bitcoin was primarily used by tech enthusiasts and libertarians who believed in the idea of a decentralized currency that operated outside the control of traditional financial institutions. Transactions were conducted on niche online forums and marketplaces, and the value of Bitcoin was negligible. However, as more people recognized the potential of this groundbreaking technology, its value began to rise, and it caught the attention of investors, entrepreneurs, and the general public.

One of the pivotal moments in the rise of cryptocurrency was the 2017 bull run. During this period, the price of Bitcoin soared from around $1,000 at the beginning of the year to nearly $20,000 by December. This meteoric rise was fueled by a combination of factors, including increased media coverage, the launch of Bitcoin futures trading, and growing interest from institutional investors. The 2017 bull run also saw the emergence of numerous altcoins, such as Ethereum, Ripple, and Litecoin, which offered different functionalities and use cases compared to Bitcoin.

This surge in interest and investment led to the development of a vibrant ecosystem of cryptocurrency exchanges, wallets, and services, making it easier for individuals to buy, sell, and store digital assets. Moreover, blockchain technology, the underlying framework of most cryptocurrencies, began to gain recognition for its potential applications beyond finance, including supply chain management, voting systems, and digital identity verification.

Despite the significant advancements and growing acceptance, the cryptocurrency market is known for its volatility. After the peak of the 2017 bull run, the market experienced a sharp correction, with the price of Bitcoin dropping by more than 80% over the following year. This boom-and-bust cycle is a recurring theme in the history of cryptocurrency, driven by speculation, regulatory developments, and technological advancements.

Blockchain Technology

At the heart of every cryptocurrency lies the blockchain, a groundbreaking technology that has the potential to reshape industries and redefine the way we think about money and value. In simple terms, a blockchain is a decentralized, distributed ledger that records transactions across a network of computers. Unlike traditional financial systems that rely on central authorities like banks, blockchains are maintained by a collective of users, ensuring transparency, security, and immutability.

Each block in the chain contains a batch of verified transactions, and once a block is added, it becomes virtually impossible to alter or remove. This tamper-proof nature of the blockchain is what makes cryptocurrencies so secure and resistant to fraud. It also eliminates the need for intermediaries, giving you greater control over your finances and reducing transaction fees.

But the blockchain is more than just a ledger; it's a platform for innovation. The technology can be used to create decentralized applications (dApps), smart contracts, and even entire decentralized autonomous organizations (DAOs). This versatility is what makes the blockchain so exciting and opens up a world of possibilities for the future.

Crypto Wallets

Much like you need a physical wallet for your cash and cards, a crypto wallet is essential for storing your digital assets. However, unlike a traditional wallet, a crypto wallet doesn't actually contain your cryptocurrencies. Instead, it stores the private and public keys that provide access to your funds on the blockchain.

Several types of wallets are available, each with its own pros and cons:

- Software Wallets: These are applications you can install on your computer or mobile device. They offer convenience and user-friendliness, making them suitable for everyday transactions.
- Hardware Wallets: These are physical devices, resembling USB drives, that store your private keys offline. They provide the

highest level of security, safeguarding your assets from hacking and malware.
- Paper Wallets: These are simply printed documents containing your private and public keys. While not as user-friendly as other wallet types, they offer a secure offline storage solution.
- Web Wallets: These are online wallets hosted by third-party providers. While convenient, they are more vulnerable to hacking and security breaches.

Selecting the right wallet depends on your specific needs and risk tolerance. If you intend to trade cryptocurrencies actively, a software wallet might be the best choice. For long-term storage and maximum security, a hardware wallet is recommended.

Crypto Exchanges

Crypto exchanges are the lifeblood of the cryptocurrency market, providing a platform for buying, selling, and trading various digital assets. They come in various forms, each catering to different needs and preferences:

- **Centralized Exchanges (CEXs):** These are the most common type of exchange, operated by companies that act as intermediaries for buyers and sellers. They offer a wide range of features, including margin trading, lending, and staking. Popular CEXs in Nigeria include Binance, Luno, and Bundle.
- **Decentralized Exchanges (DEXs):** These operate on the blockchain, without a central authority. They offer greater privacy and security but can be less user-friendly and have lower liquidity than CEXs.
- **Peer-to-Peer (P2P) Exchanges:** These platforms connect buyers and sellers directly, allowing them to negotiate prices and terms. P2P exchanges are popular in countries with strict regulations or limited access to traditional banking services.

When selecting an exchange, consider factors like security, fees, liquidity, supported cryptocurrencies, user experience, and customer support. It's also important to research the exchange's reputation and regulatory compliance.

Major Cryptocurrencies

The crypto market is vast and diverse, with thousands of different cryptocurrencies competing for attention. However, some have emerged as clear leaders, each with its own unique value proposition:

- **Bitcoin (BTC):** The original and most valuable cryptocurrency, often referred to as "digital gold." Bitcoin is known for its limited supply, decentralized nature, and potential as a store of value.
- **Ethereum (ETH):** A versatile platform for building decentralized applications (dApps) and smart contracts. Ethereum is the second-largest cryptocurrency by market capitalization and is at the forefront of the decentralized finance (DeFi) revolution.
- **Ripple (XRP):** A cryptocurrency designed for fast and efficient cross-border payments. Ripple is often used by banks and financial institutions to facilitate international transactions.
- **Litecoin (LTC):** A peer-to-peer cryptocurrency and a close competitor to

Bitcoin. Litecoin is often referred to as "silver to Bitcoin's gold" and is known for its faster transaction confirmation times.

These are just a few examples of the many cryptocurrencies available in the market. Remember to conduct thorough research and understand the risks before investing in any digital asset.

Altcoins

Beyond Bitcoin and Ethereum, there exists a vast universe of alternative cryptocurrencies, collectively known as altcoins. These digital assets offer a wide array of features and use cases, catering to niche markets and specific needs.

- **Stablecoins:** These are cryptocurrencies designed to maintain a stable value, usually pegged to a fiat currency like the US dollar. Stablecoins offer a safe haven from the volatility of other cryptocurrencies and are often used for trading and as a medium of exchange. The most common is Tether USDT.

- **Privacy Coins:** These cryptocurrencies prioritize anonymity and privacy, using advanced cryptography to obscure transaction details. Popular privacy coins include Monero and Zcash.
- **Utility Tokens:** These are digital assets that provide access to a specific product or service within a blockchain ecosystem.
- **Security Tokens:** These are digital representations of traditional securities like stocks, bonds, or real estate. Security tokens offer fractional ownership and greater liquidity compared to traditional assets.

The world of altcoins is constantly evolving, with new projects emerging regularly. It's a high-risk, high-reward environment that requires careful research and due diligence.

Market Cycles

The cryptocurrency market is renowned for its dramatic price fluctuations, commonly referred to as market cycles. These cycles are characterized by periods of rapid growth (bull markets) followed by periods of decline (bear markets).

Grasping market cycles is essential for making well-informed investment decisions. By recognizing the different stages of the cycle, you can identify potential opportunities and minimize risks.

- Accumulation Phase: During this stage, prices are low, and smart investors begin accumulating assets.
- Markup Phase: Prices rise as more investors enter the market, driven by FOMO (fear of missing out) and positive sentiment.
- Distribution Phase: Prices reach their peak, and early investors start taking profits.
- Markdown Phase: Prices fall as the market corrects, often leading to panic selling and a return to the accumulation phase.

These cycles can be influenced by a variety of factors, including technological advancements, regulatory changes, macroeconomic events, and investor sentiment.

Bull Run 2024

Chapter 2

Bull Market Mechanics

In this chapter, we'll go into the complex workings of bull markets, exploring the key drivers that propel prices upward and create a frenzy of excitement among investors. We'll examine the fundamental principles of supply and demand, the impact of technological advancements and regulatory changes, and the crucial role of market sentiment. By understanding these forces, you'll gain valuable insights into how to identify early signs of a bull market and make informed investment decisions.

What Drives Bull Runs?

Supply and Demand

The core of any market is rooted in the basic economic concept of supply and demand. In the realm of cryptocurrencies, the constrained supply of numerous crypto assets, paired with growing demand, generates a potent upward force on prices.

Take Bitcoin as an illustration: it has a maximum supply cap of 21 million coins. As awareness spreads and more individuals invest in Bitcoin, demand escalates while the supply remains constant, naturally driving up the price. This principle of scarcity extends to many other cryptocurrencies, making the interplay of supply and demand a crucial element in propelling bull markets.

It's important to note, however, that supply and demand are not fixed forces. They are continuously shaped by various factors, including investor sentiment, market developments, and broader economic trends. Grasping these dynamics is essential for anticipating market shifts and making well-timed investment choices.

Technological Advancements

Technological advancements play a crucial role in fueling bull markets. Fresh developments in blockchain technology, such as scalability solutions, enhanced security protocols, and innovative use cases, can significantly boost investor confidence and draw new participants to the market.

For instance, the emergence of decentralized finance (DeFi) in 2020 and 2021, with its groundbreaking financial products and services, was a key driver of the previous bull run. As blockchain technology continues to advance, we can anticipate further breakthroughs that could ignite new waves of adoption and push prices higher.

Regulatory Shifts

Government policies can exert a profound influence on the cryptocurrency market. Favorable regulatory developments, such as clear guidelines for taxation and investor protection, can enhance confidence and encourage institutional investment. This is evident in regions like the European Union, where the Markets in Crypto-Assets (MiCA) regulation has established a comprehensive framework for crypto businesses, fostering a more secure environment for investors.

Conversely, strict regulations or outright prohibitions can hinder innovation and dampen market sentiment. We've observed this in countries like China, where a crackdown on crypto mining and trading prompted a significant exodus of crypto businesses and investors.

The United States, a major player in the global crypto landscape, is currently grappling with its own regulatory challenges. The Securities and Exchange Commission (SEC) and the Commodity Futures Trading Commission (CFTC) are both asserting jurisdiction over the crypto market, leading to uncertainty and potential conflicts. The resolution of this regulatory power struggle could have far-reaching consequences for the future of crypto in the US and beyond.

Market Sentiment

Market sentiment, often driven by fear and greed, plays a crucial role in driving bull markets. When investors are optimistic and confident, they are more likely to buy and hold cryptocurrencies, pushing prices higher. Conversely, negative sentiment can lead to panic selling and a rapid decline in prices.

News events, social media trends, and the actions of influential figures can all sway market sentiment. For example, Elon Musk's tweets about Dogecoin in 2021 had a significant impact on the price of the meme-inspired cryptocurrency. Understanding how market sentiment works and recognizing the signs of shifting tides is essential for successful crypto investing.

Identifying Early Signs of a Bull Market

While it's impossible to precisely forecast the beginning of a bull market, several early indicators can suggest a potential upward trend:

- Elevated Trading Volume: A notable increase in trading activity across major exchanges may signal rising interest and demand for digital currencies.
- Positive News and Technological Advancements: Favorable news reports,

regulatory endorsements, or technological innovations can ignite optimism and draw in new investors.

- Breakout from Key Resistance Levels: Technical analysis tools such as charts and indicators can reveal when prices are breaking through significant resistance levels, potentially signaling the onset of a new upward trajectory.
- Increasing Social Media Traction: A surge in discussions and positive sentiment on social media platforms can serve as an early sign of growing interest and adoption.

Basic Technical Analysis for Interpreting Charts

Technical analysis is a powerful tool for understanding market trends and predicting future price movements. While it's a complex discipline with countless indicators and patterns, understanding a few basic concepts can significantly enhance your investment strategy.

Support and Resistance Levels: These are price levels where buying or selling pressure is expected to be strong. Identifying these levels can help you anticipate potential turning points in the market.

Support Level:

The horizontal line at the bottom is the support level. It represents a price level where buying interest is strong enough to prevent the price from falling further. In the diagram, we can see that the price has touched this level multiple times but has not fallen below it. This suggests that buyers are willing to step in and purchase the asset at this price, creating a "floor" for the price.

Resistance Level:

The horizontal line at the top is the resistance level. It represents a price level where selling pressure is strong enough to prevent the price from rising further. In the diagram, we can see that the price has attempted to break through this level multiple times but has failed. This suggests that sellers are willing to unload their assets at this price, creating a "ceiling" for the price.

Interpretation:

Support and resistance levels are crucial concepts in technical analysis, as they can help traders and investors identify potential turning points in the market. Here's how this diagram can be interpreted:

- **Potential Trading Strategies:**
    - **Buy:** Traders might consider buying when the price approaches the support level, anticipating that it will bounce back up.
    - **Sell:** Traders might consider selling when the price approaches the resistance level, anticipating that it will fall back down.

- o **Breakout:** If the price breaks through the resistance level with strong volume, it could signal a bullish trend and potential for further upward movement.
- o **Breakdown:** If the price falls below the support level with strong volume, it could signal a bearish trend and potential for further downward movement.
- **Price Range:** The area between the support and resistance levels can be seen as a trading range. The price may oscillate within this range for a period until it either breaks out or breaks down.

Important Considerations:

1. Support and resistance levels are not fixed and can change over time as market conditions shift.
2. It's important to look for confirmation from other technical indicators or chart patterns before making trading decisions based solely on support and resistance levels.

3. Always use proper risk management techniques, such as stop-loss orders, to protect your capital in case the market moves against your expectations.

Trendlines: These are lines drawn on a chart that connect a series of highs or lows, indicating the direction of the trend.

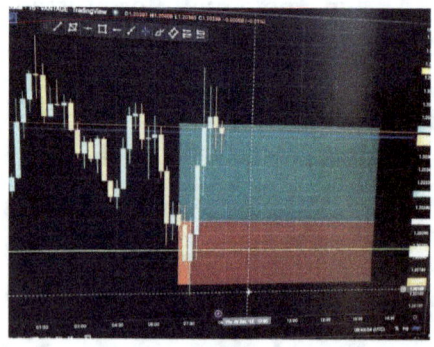

The above image shows a candlestick chart with a significant trendline. It seems to be a support-turned-resistance level.

- **Support-Turned-Resistance:** Initially, the green zone acted as a support level, as the price bounced off it several times. However, when the price broke below the green zone, it flipped and started acting as a

resistance level. This is evident in the chart as the price attempted to move back into the green zone (old support) but was rejected and pushed back down.
- **Breakdown and Retest:** The red zone indicates the area where the price broke down from the initial support level. The candlesticks within this zone represent the price attempting to retest the breakdown level but failing to do so. This further confirms the change in the trendline's role from support to resistance.

Overall, this chart illustrates the concept of support and resistance levels and how they can change roles depending on market behavior. It's a classic example of how traders use trendlines to identify potential entry and exit points in the market

Moving Averages: These are lines that smooth out price data over a specified period, helping to filter out noise and identify the underlying trend.

The chart shows the Bitcoin (BTC) price in USDT (Tether) pairing over a period of time. The chart has two Moving Averages (MA) applied:

- **MA (9, close, 0):** This is a 9-period simple moving average calculated using the closing prices of the last 9 candlesticks. It's a short-term MA that reacts more quickly to price changes, making it useful for identifying short-term trends.
- **MA (20, close, 0):** This is a 20-period simple moving average, also calculated using the closing prices of the last 20 candlesticks. As a longer-term MA, it smooths out price fluctuations more than

the 9-period MA, giving a better indication of the overall trend.

Interpretation:

1. **Trend:** The overall trend on the chart is bearish. Both moving averages are sloping downwards, indicating that the average price of Bitcoin has been decreasing over time.
2. **Crossover (Death Cross):** Around the beginning of November, the 9-day MA crossed below the 20-day MA. This is known as a "death cross" and is generally considered a bearish signal, suggesting that the downward trend may continue.
3. **Price Action Relative to MAs:** The price of Bitcoin has been trading below both moving averages for most of the charted period, further confirming the bearish sentiment. Occasionally, the price has tried to move above the MAs, but these attempts have been short-lived, and the price has been pulled back down.
4. **Possible Support Level:** There is a horizontal line drawn around the 40,000

USDT mark. This could be interpreted as a potential support level, where buyers might step in to prevent further price declines. However, the price has recently broken below this level, which could indicate a weakening of support.

Potential Interpretation for Traders:

- **Short-term:** The current trend and indicators suggest a bearish outlook in the short term. Traders might consider shorting Bitcoin or avoiding long positions.
- **Long-term:** It's important to note that this is just a snapshot in time. Long-term investors might want to watch for potential signs of a trend reversal, such as a sustained price increase above the moving averages or a "golden cross" (the 9-day MA crossing above the 20-day MA). However, it's crucial to conduct thorough research and consider other factors before making any investment decisions.

By combining these tools with fundamental analysis and an understanding of market sentiment, you can develop a well-rounded approach to crypto investing and traversing the exciting world of bull markets with confidence.

Bull Run 2024

Chapter 3

Risk and Reward

Do you know that Bitcoin, the pioneering and most renowned cryptocurrency, underwent a jaw-dropping 99.9996% plunge from its peak value in 2011? This serves as a potent reminder of the extreme price swings that can impact the cryptocurrency market. However, alongside these risks lie extraordinary opportunities for those who can adeptly navigate this thrilling new financial landscape. In this section, we'll delve into the intricacies of risk and reward within the crypto sphere, arming you with the insights and tactics necessary to make well-informed choices and protect your investments.

The crypto market's volatility is both its most alluring and intimidating feature. While it offers the potential for astronomical gains, it also presents the risk of substantial losses. Understanding this duality is crucial for any crypto investor.

Let's break down the key components of risk and reward in cryptocurrency:

1. Market Volatility: Crypto prices can fluctuate wildly in short periods. This volatility can be attributed to factors such as regulatory news, technological advancements, market sentiment, and even social media trends. While this volatility can lead to significant profits, it can also result in severe losses if not managed properly.

2. Regulatory Risk: The regulatory landscape for cryptocurrencies is still evolving. Changes in government policies or regulations can have a profound impact on the value and utility of cryptocurrencies. Staying informed about regulatory developments in your jurisdiction and globally is essential.

3. Technological Risk: The blockchain technology underlying cryptocurrencies is still relatively new and evolving. There's always the risk of bugs, hacks, or fundamental flaws in the technology being discovered. Moreover, newer, more efficient technologies could potentially make current cryptocurrencies obsolete.

4. Liquidity Risk: Some cryptocurrencies, especially newer or less popular ones, may have low trading volumes. This can make it difficult to buy or sell large amounts without significantly affecting the price.

5. Counterparty Risk: When using centralized exchanges or participating in DeFi protocols, there's always a risk that the other party (the exchange, the protocol, or other users) might not fulfill their obligations.

On the reward side, cryptocurrencies offer several potential benefits:

1. High Returns: Despite the risks, cryptocurrencies have historically offered some of the highest returns of any asset class. Early Bitcoin investors, for example, have seen returns in the millions of percent.

2. Portfolio Diversification: Cryptocurrencies often move independently of traditional financial markets, making them a potential tool for portfolio diversification.

3. Financial Innovation: Cryptocurrencies and blockchain technology are enabling new financial services and products, particularly in the realm of decentralized finance (DeFi). These innovations offer new ways to earn yields, access loans, and participate in global finance.

4. Democratization of Finance: Cryptocurrencies provide access to financial services for unbanked and underbanked populations worldwide. They also allow for peer-to-peer transactions without the need for intermediaries.

5. Technological Revolution: Investing in cryptocurrencies is not just about financial gains; it's also about participating in a technological revolution that has the potential to reshape various industries.

Investing vs. Trading:

Before we dive into risk management, it's essential to distinguish between two primary approaches to engaging with the crypto market: investing and trading.

Investing:

Cryptocurrency investors often adopt a long-term perspective. They have faith in the underlying technology and the enduring potential of cryptocurrencies to revolutionize the financial sector. These individuals typically acquire and retain assets for extended durations, often spanning years, anticipating value appreciation over time.

Advantages:

1. Prospect of substantial returns: Historically, cryptocurrencies have demonstrated the potential for exponential growth, with some early adopters reaping considerable rewards.
2. Low-maintenance approach: Investing demands less active oversight and time commitment compared to trading.
3. Compounding benefits: As your investments expand over time, the gains can accumulate, potentially leading to even greater returns.

Disadvantages:

1. Extreme volatility: Crypto markets are infamous for their instability, with prices fluctuating dramatically. This can result in significant losses if one is unprepared for the market's ups and downs.
2. 2. Extended time frame: It may require years for your investments to reach their full potential, necessitating patience and discipline.
3. Risk of complete loss: While the potential for gains is substantial, there's also a possibility of losing your entire investment if a project fails or the market crashes.

Trading:

Crypto traders adopt a more proactive stance, aiming to profit from short-term price movements. They employ various strategies, such as technical analysis and chart patterns, to identify buying and selling opportunities.

Advantages:

1. Potential for rapid profits: Skilled traders can exploit market volatility and generate significant profits in a brief period.
2. Adaptability: Trading allows you to adjust to changing market conditions and capitalize on both rising and falling prices.
3. Thrill and challenge: For some, the fast-paced nature of trading offers an exhilarating challenge and a sense of achievement.

Disadvantages:

1. High risk: Trading is inherently perilous, and even seasoned traders can incur substantial losses.
2. Time-intensive: Successful trading requires constant market monitoring and the ability to make swift decisions.
3. Emotional impact: The psychological highs and lows of trading can be exhausting and lead to impulsive choices.

Risk Management

In the cryptocurrency market, effective risk management is essential for both investors and traders. Several key strategies can help safeguard your capital:

- Asset Allocation: Avoid concentrating your funds in a single cryptocurrency. Instead, distribute your investments across various digital assets to mitigate the impact of individual asset volatility.
- Investment Sizing: Establish limits on the amount of capital you're comfortable risking for each trade or investment opportunity. This approach prevents overexposure and protects your portfolio from significant losses.
- Downside Protection: Implement automatic sell orders at predetermined price levels to cap potential losses. This strategy is vital for navigating the unpredictable nature of cryptocurrency markets.
- Profit Realization: Define target prices at which you'll liquidate assets to secure gains.

This tactic helps prevent the common pitfall of holding onto assets too long during bullish market conditions.

- Market Awareness: Continuously monitor the latest developments and news in the cryptocurrency sphere. Staying informed enables you to make well-reasoned decisions and anticipate both potential risks and promising opportunities.

Realistic Expectations: The Key to Long-Term Success

The appeal of cryptocurrency investment stems from tales of rapid wealth accumulation and the enticing prospect of financial independence. However, it's vital to temper your expectations with reality and approach the market with a clear grasp of both potential gains and inherent dangers.

Cryptocurrency markets are susceptible to cycles of hype, where enthusiasm and speculation drive asset values to unsustainable heights, followed by sharp downturns. These patterns can foster a deceptive sense of security and promote rash decision-making. To cultivate realistic expectations, it's crucial to recognize that:

- Not all investments will yield positive returns: Despite thorough research and careful analysis, some investments will inevitably underperform or fail completely.
- Market entry timing is critical: Joining the market at the zenith of a hype cycle can result in substantial losses when the bubble eventually bursts.
- Historical performance doesn't guarantee future success: The fact that a cryptocurrency has performed well previously doesn't ensure continued positive results.

Common Mistakes and Misconceptions

To effectively maneuver through the cryptocurrency market, it's essential to steer clear of widespread traps and misunderstandings:

- FOMO (Fear of Missing Out): The fear of missing out on potential gains can lead to impulsive buying decisions, frequently at inflated valuations.

- Neglecting risk management: A lot of investors overlook risk management tactics, such as portfolio diversification and implementing stop-loss orders, exposing their entire investment to potential loss.

- Blindly following trends: Pursuing the most recent fads or overhyped projects without thorough investigation can result in expensive errors.

- Overconfidence: The belief that one can consistently outperform the market or forecast price fluctuations with absolute certainty is a formula for failure.

- Emotion-driven investing: Allowing sentiments like fear and greed to govern your investment choices can lead to irrational actions and overlooked prospects.

Setting Realistic Goals and Managing Expectations

To establish realistic expectations and effectively manage your emotions, consider the following advice:

- Define clear financial objectives: Identify your reasons for investing in cryptocurrencies and your desired outcomes. Having well-defined goals will help you maintain focus and make rational choices.
- Craft a long-term investment strategy: Avoid the temptation of get-rich-quick schemes. Instead, concentrate on constructing a diverse portfolio and holding your investments for an extended period.
- Perform comprehensive due diligence: Prior to investing in any cryptocurrency, investigate the project thoroughly, including the team behind it, the underlying technology, and its market potential.

- Limit your investment to what you can afford to lose: Only invest funds that you can bear to lose without compromising your financial stability.
- Diversify your investment portfolio: Distribute your investments across various cryptocurrencies to minimize your exposure to the volatility of any single asset.
- Employ risk management techniques: Implement stop-loss and take-profit orders to safeguard your capital and secure profits.
- Stay well-informed: Keep abreast of the latest news and developments in the cryptocurrency market to make educated decisions.

Dedicate time and effort to research, cultivate patience, and practice sound risk management. Approach the crypto market as a marathon rather than a sprint, and your financial success will become a reality.

Bull Run 2024

Chapter 4

Market Analysis

Did you know that there are over 10,000 cryptocurrencies in existence today? Despite this diversity, Bitcoin and Ethereum continue to dominate, collectively representing over half of the total market value.

This vast and dynamic market presents both opportunities and challenges for investors. In this chapter, we'll analyze the present-day cryptocurrency world, explore expert predictions for 2024, and identify the key catalysts and roadblocks that could shape the market's trajectory.

What's Happened Since the Last Bull Run?

Since the euphoric highs of the 2020-2021 bull run, the crypto market has experienced a significant correction. Bitcoin, which peaked at nearly $69,000 in November 2021, is now hovering around $61,911 as at 3rd August, 2024. Ethereum has also seen a similar decline, though it remains the dominant platform for decentralized applications (dApps) and smart contracts.

This correction is not unexpected, as bull runs are often followed by periods of consolidation and price adjustment. However, it's important to note that the underlying technology and fundamentals of the crypto market remain strong. Institutional adoption continues to grow, with major players like BlackRock and Fidelity Investments launching crypto-related products and services. Financial institutions like JPMorgan and Goldman Sachs have increased their exposure to crypto assets, offering clients access to Bitcoin and other cryptocurrencies.

Countries like El Salvador have embraced Bitcoin as legal tender, while the U.S. and EU have been working on comprehensive regulatory frameworks to integrate cryptocurrencies into their financial systems. Retail interest also remains high, with a growing number of individuals recognizing the potential of digital assets.

2024 Predictions: What the Experts Are Saying

While predicting the future is always a risky endeavor, many experts and analysts believe that 2024 could be a year of resurgence for the crypto market. According to Cathie Wood of ARK Invest, the increasing institutional interest and technological advancements in blockchain could propel Bitcoin to new all-time highs. Similarly, Mike Novogratz, CEO of Galaxy Digital, has emphasized the growing role of decentralized finance (DeFi) and non-fungible tokens (NFTs) in driving market growth. Several factors support this optimistic outlook:

- **Bitcoin Halving:** The Bitcoin which happened in April, 2024, reducing the rate at which new Bitcoins are created and potentially leading to a supply shock that could drive prices higher.
- **Increased Adoption:** The growing adoption of cryptocurrencies by individuals, businesses, and even governments is

expected to continue, increasing demand and driving prices higher.

- **Technological Advancements:** Ongoing developments in blockchain technology, such as scalability solutions and improved security, could make cryptocurrencies more attractive to both investors and users.
- **Regulatory Clarity:** As governments around the world grapple with how to regulate cryptocurrencies, clearer and more favorable regulations could boost investor confidence and accelerate adoption.

However, it's important to note that not all predictions are rosy. Some analysts caution that the market could face further corrections or even a prolonged bear market before the next bull run. The unpredictable nature of the crypto market makes it essential to approach any prediction with a healthy dose of skepticism and to always conduct thorough research before making any investment decisions.

Potential Catalysts and Roadblocks

Several factors could act as catalysts for a 2024 bull run:

- **ETF Approvals:** The approval of Bitcoin exchange-traded funds (ETFs) in major markets like the United States could open the doors to a flood of institutional investment.
- **Global Economic Instability:** Rising inflation, geopolitical tensions, and economic uncertainty could drive investors towards alternative assets like Bitcoin, seen as a hedge against inflation and a store of value.
- **DeFi Growth:** The continued growth of decentralized finance (DeFi), with its innovative financial products and services, could attract more users and capital to the crypto market.
- **Web3 Development:** The development of Web3, a decentralized internet powered by

blockchain technology, could revolutionize various industries and create new opportunities for cryptocurrencies.
- **Donald Trump's Support:** Donald Trump has occasionally voiced support for cryptocurrencies, notably tweeting, "Do not sell your Bitcoin; it's a great investment." His potential election victory could lead to more crypto-friendly policies, further bolstering market sentiment.

Roadblocks

Despite the potential catalysts, several roadblocks could hinder the crypto market's progress in 2024:

- **Regulatory Hurdles:** Uncertain or unfavorable regulations could stifle innovation and deter investors. Harsh regulatory actions in key markets like the U.S. or China can stifle innovation and reduce market activity.
- **Security Concerns:** Hacks, scams, and other security breaches could erode investor confidence and slow down adoption.

- **Volatility:** The inherent volatility of the crypto market could deter risk-averse investors and create opportunities for market manipulation.
- **Environmental Concerns:** The energy consumption associated with Bitcoin mining has raised concerns about the environmental impact of cryptocurrencies, potentially leading to negative public sentiment and regulatory action.
- **Economic Downturns:** Global economic instability or recessions can lead to reduced risk appetite among investors, negatively impacting crypto prices.

The crypto market is ever-changing, it's essential to maintain a balanced perspective. While the potential for a 2024 bull run is real, it's equally important to be aware of the challenges and risks involved. By staying informed, conducting thorough research, and managing risk effectively, you can position yourself to take advantage of the opportunities that lie ahead.

Bull Run 2024

Chapter 5

Investment Strategies

Greetings, crypto explorers! If you've ventured this far, you've likely already dipped into the cryptocurrency pool, perhaps even taken a few laps. But are you ready to build an ark that can weather any storm? A well-diversified crypto portfolio isn't merely about possessing various digital assets; it's about positioning yourself strategically to ride the waves rather than being overwhelmed by them.

Do you know?

- As at mid-2024, Bitcoin continues to dominate, representing over 40% of the total cryptocurrency market capitalization. Does this imply it's the sole asset worth owning? Not at all! While this dominance highlights Bitcoin's crucial role, it also points to potential growth opportunities in alternative cryptocurrencies.

- Mainstream financial adoption is ongoing as prominent financial institutions such as BlackRock and Fidelity are now entering the crypto sphere. This isn't just a stamp of approval; it's accelerating adoption, potentially boosting demand and valuations.
- Decentralized finance (DeFi) platforms have now secured over $50 billion in assets. These platforms introduce innovative financial services like lending, borrowing, and yield generation, creating novel avenues for crypto investors to earn returns.

These facts aren't mere trivia; they're indicators of the opportunities and challenges present in the cryptocurrency landscape. Let's use them to guide our journey.

Assessing Risk Tolerance and Financial Objectives

Before you begin accumulating satoshis or pursuing the next potential breakout coin, take a moment for self-reflection. How much risk are you comfortable with? Are you an adrenaline junkie ready for a wild ride, or do you prefer a more gradual ascent? What are your financial aspirations? Are you investing for your golden years, saving for a property, or simply aiming to outpace inflation?

Your responses to these queries will inform your asset distribution. A high risk tolerance might lead you towards a portfolio with a larger proportion of altcoins and perhaps even some meme coins. A more cautious approach might favor a greater allocation to Bitcoin and stablecoins.

Dollar-Cost Averaging (DCA) vs. Lump-Sum Investing

Let's discuss investment strategies. Two common approaches are periodic investment and one-time investment.

DCA: This method involves investing a set amount at regular intervals, regardless of price fluctuations. This approach helps smooth out volatility, potentially reducing your average purchase price over time. It's particularly suitable for newcomers and those who prefer a structured, low-maintenance approach.

Example: You invest $100 in Bitcoin weekly. When prices are high, you acquire less Bitcoin. When prices are low, you acquire more.

Lump-Sum Investing: This strategy involves investing a substantial sum all at once. It's a higher-risk approach that can yield greater rewards if timed correctly, but also greater losses if the market experiences a downturn.

Example: You receive a $5,000 windfall and decide to invest the entire amount in Ethereum at its current price.

Which strategy suits you best? It depends on your risk appetite and market outlook. If you believe a bull market is imminent, a one-time investment might be appealing. However, if you're uncertain about future market movements, periodic investment offers a more conservative approach.

Spot Trading vs. Derivatives

Consider direct asset purchase as acquiring the actual cryptocurrency, such as Bitcoin or Ethereum. It's the most straightforward investment method, but it also means you're fully exposed to price movements.

Financial derivatives, conversely, are instruments that derive their value from an underlying asset. Think of them as wagering on the future price of a cryptocurrency without actually owning it.

- **Futures contracts:** These allow you to agree to buy or sell a cryptocurrency at a predetermined price on a future date.
- **Options contracts:** These provide you with the right, but not the obligation, to buy or sell a cryptocurrency at a specific price by a certain date.

Derivatives can be potent tools for mitigating risk and amplifying gains, but they're also more intricate and carry higher risks. They're not for the faint of heart!

Building a Diversified Crypto Portfolio

Let's illustrate with a sample portfolio based on a moderate risk tolerance:

- **Bitcoin (BTC):** 40%
- **Ethereum (ETH):** 30%
- **Binance Coin (BNB):** 10%
- **Altcoin Basket (e.g., Solana, Cardano, Polygon):** 15%
- **Stablecoin (e.g., USDT, USDC):** 5%

This is just a starting point. Your ideal portfolio will depend on your individual circumstances and research.

Here are three more sample portfolios with varying risk tolerances, plus two additional portfolios incorporating meme coins:

1. Conservative Portfolio (Low Risk):

- **Bitcoin (BTC):** 60%
- **Ethereum (ETH):** 20%
- **Stablecoins (USDT, USDC):** 20%

This portfolio prioritizes stability and capital preservation, with a significant allocation to Bitcoin as the most established cryptocurrency and stablecoins to hedge against volatility.

2. **Balanced Portfolio (Moderate Risk):**

- **Bitcoin (BTC):** 40%
- **Ethereum (ETH):** 25%
- **Binance Coin (BNB):** 10%
- **Altcoin Basket (Solana, Cardano, Polygon):** 20%
- **Stablecoin (USDT):** 5%

This portfolio offers a balance between potential growth and risk mitigation. It includes a mix of established and emerging cryptocurrencies, with a small allocation to stablecoins for liquidity.

3. **Aggressive Portfolio (High Risk):**

- **Bitcoin (BTC):** 20%
- **Ethereum (ETH):** 20%
- **Altcoin Basket (Layer 1s, Layer 2s, DeFi Tokens):** 50%

- **Meme Coins (Dogecoin, Shiba Inu):** 10%

This portfolio is designed for those seeking high potential returns, but also willing to accept high volatility. It includes a larger allocation to altcoins and even a small portion to meme coins, which can experience significant price swings.

Meme Coin Portfolios:

1. Meme Coin Enthusiast:

- **Dogecoin (DOGE):** 40%
- **Shiba Inu (SHIB):** 30%
- **PEPE:** 20%
- **Other Meme Coins (e.g., FLOKI, ELON):** 10%

This portfolio is purely speculative and not recommended for most investors. It's designed for those who enjoy the fun and community aspect of meme coins, but also understand the extreme risks involved.

2. Meme Coin Diversification:

- **Bitcoin (BTC):** 50%
- **Ethereum (ETH):** 20%
- **Dogecoin (DOGE):** 15%
- **Shiba Inu (SHIB):** 15%

This portfolio combines a core of established cryptocurrencies with a smaller allocation to meme coins. It aims to balance potential growth with some level of risk management.

Important Note: Meme coins are highly volatile and should only be considered with a small portion of your overall portfolio, if at all. Do your own research and understand the risks before investing in any meme coin.

Bull Run 2024

Chapter 6

Emerging Trends

While Bitcoin and Ethereum continue to hold the crypto spotlight, a new wave of innovation is surging beneath the surface, poised to redefine the digital landscape. Decentralized finance (DeFi), non-fungible tokens (NFTs), and the metaverse are not just buzzwords; they're rapidly evolving ecosystems that could shape the trajectory of the 2024 bull run.

DeFi

Picture a financial world where you're not just a customer, but a participant. That's the promise of DeFi, a network of decentralized applications built on blockchain technology. These applications offer financial services like lending, borrowing, trading, and yield farming, all without intermediaries like banks or brokers.

The numbers speak volumes:

- **Total Value Locked (TVL):** The total value of assets locked in DeFi protocols has surged past $100 billion, indicating the growing trust and adoption of these platforms.
- **Yield Farming Frenzy:** Investors are flocking to yield farming, a process where they lend out their crypto assets to earn rewards. Some platforms offer annual percentage yields (APYs) in the triple digits, albeit with higher risks.

But DeFi isn't just about chasing high yields. It's about empowering individuals, fostering financial inclusion, and democratizing access to financial services.

DeFi is more than just a buzzword; it's a financial revolution in the making. Here's a glimpse into some of the leading DeFi platforms:

- **Aave:** A decentralized lending and borrowing platform where users can earn interest on their deposits or borrow crypto assets using their holdings as collateral.

- **MakerDAO:** The creator of DAI, a decentralized stablecoin pegged to the US dollar. MakerDAO allows users to generate DAI by locking up other cryptocurrencies as collateral.
- **Uniswap:** A decentralized exchange (DEX) where users can trade cryptocurrencies directly from their wallets without the need for a centralized intermediary.
- **Curve Finance:** A DEX specializing in stablecoin trading, offering low slippage and efficient swaps between different stablecoins.
- **Compound:** Another lending and borrowing platform similar to Aave, but with a different interest rate model.
- **PancakeSwap:** A popular DEX on the Binance Smart Chain, known for its high yields and diverse selection of tokens.
- **SushiSwap:** A fork of Uniswap with additional features like yield farming and staking rewards.

NFTs

Non-fungible tokens, or NFTs, are unique digital assets that represent ownership of a specific item or piece of content. While they initially gained fame through digital art sales, NFTs are now being used for a wide range of applications, including:

- **Gaming Assets:** NFTs can represent in-game items like characters, weapons, or virtual land, giving players true ownership and the ability to trade them freely.
- **Collectibles:** From sports memorabilia to virtual real estate, NFTs are transforming the collectibles market, creating new opportunities for creators and collectors alike.
- **Music and Entertainment:** Musicians are releasing albums as NFTs, giving fans a unique way to support their favorite artists and access exclusive content.

The NFT market is still in its early stages, but its potential is vast. As more creators and brands embrace NFTs, we can expect to see a surge in innovation and adoption.

The NFT space is buzzing with activity, and several marketplaces have emerged as go-to destinations for creators and collectors:

- **OpenSea:** The largest NFT marketplace, offering a wide range of digital assets, including art, collectibles, gaming items, and more.
- **Rarible:** A community-owned NFT marketplace where creators can mint and sell their own NFTs, and collectors can discover unique pieces.
- **SuperRare:** A curated platform focused on high-quality digital art, featuring exclusive drops and limited edition collections.
- **Foundation:** Another curated platform known for its emphasis on artistic expression and experimental projects.
- **Nifty Gateway:** A popular platform for NFT drops, featuring collaborations with renowned artists and brands.

- **Binance NFT:** The NFT marketplace launched by Binance, offering a wide range of NFTs and integration with the Binance ecosystem.

These marketplaces offer different experiences and cater to various niches within the NFT space. Whether you're a seasoned collector or a curious newcomer, there's a marketplace out there for you.

The Metaverse

Can you think of a virtual world where you can work, play, socialize, and even own properties? That's the concept behind the metaverse, a shared, immersive digital space that's gaining traction thanks to advancements in virtual reality (VR) and augmented reality (AR) technologies.

The metaverse is not just a gaming platform; it's a new frontier for social interaction, commerce, and creativity. Brands like Nike and Coca-Cola are already experimenting with virtual experiences in the metaverse, while platforms like Decentraland and The Sandbox are allowing users to buy and develop virtual land.

How These Trends Could Shape the 2024 Bull Run

DeFi, NFTs, and the metaverse are not isolated phenomena; they're interconnected pieces of a larger puzzle that's reshaping the digital landscape. Here's how they could influence the 2024 bull run:

- **Increased Demand:** As these technologies gain mainstream adoption, they could attract a new wave of investors, driving up demand for cryptocurrencies and potentially fueling a bull run.
- **New Investment Opportunities:** DeFi platforms, NFT marketplaces, and metaverse projects offer a plethora of new investment opportunities, from yield farming to virtual real estate.
- **Innovation and Growth:** The rapid pace of innovation in these sectors could create a positive feedback loop, attracting more developers, entrepreneurs, and investors, further fueling growth.

Seizing the Opportunities

To capitalize on these trends, consider:

- **Researching DeFi Projects:** Explore different DeFi platforms and protocols, understand their risks and rewards, and consider participating in yield farming or liquidity providing.
- **Investing in NFTs:** If you're passionate about art, gaming, or collectibles, consider investing in NFTs from reputable creators or projects.
- **Exploring the Metaverse:** Participate in virtual events, explore virtual worlds, and consider investing in virtual land or other metaverse assets.

Telegram Based Play-to-Earn earn Games and Their Tokens

Telegram's massive user base and mini-app capabilities have made it a fertile ground for play-to-earn (P2E) games, attracting millions of players eager to earn crypto while having fun. The first prominent and popular P2E game on Telegram was Notcoin, a simple yet engaging game that allowed users to "mine" Notcoin tokens by tapping on an animated coin within the chat interface.

Despite its initial memecoin status and lack of a defined purpose, Notcoin quickly gained traction, amassing over 5 million players within a week of its official launch on January 1, 2024. Its popularity stemmed from its simplicity, accessibility, and integration with Telegram, making it an easy entry point for beginners into the world of blockchain and cryptocurrency.

While Notcoin's mining phase has ended, and the token was airdropped to the community in mid-April 2024, with participants making hundreds to thousands of dollars, its legacy lives on. As of August 7, 2024, Notcoin is trading at $0.013, a testament to its enduring appeal and the potential of Telegram-based P2E games.

Notcoin's journey highlights the potential for Telegram to become a major hub for P2E gaming, offering a vast audience and a user-friendly platform for developers. As more games emerge, we can expect to see a surge in innovation and adoption, further blurring the lines between gaming and crypto.

Hamster Kombat

Hamster Kombat is a unique play-to-earn game hosted on Telegram, designed to introduce the masses to the world of Web3. Launched around March 2024, with over 250 million players worldwide, it's the largest crypto game ever, and it aims to onboard a billion more users to the blockchain.

In Hamster Kombat, players become crypto exchange CEOs. They start by tapping the screen to earn in-game coins. These coins can then be used to purchase profitable cards, each generating passive income per hour. By strategically buying and upgrading cards, players can maximize their earnings.

The game also features daily challenges, including a Daily Combo and a Daily Cipher. The Daily Combo involves buying three specific cards to earn a whopping 5 million coins. The Daily Cipher is a puzzle that, when solved, rewards players with a key. These keys unlock various benefits and rewards, especially during airdrop distributions.

Hamster Kombat's playground section offers mini-games where players can earn coupon codes. These codes can be redeemed for keys, further enhancing the rewards and benefits players can unlock.

A key aspect of Hamster Kombat is its upcoming airdrop, which promises to be the largest in crypto history. This airdrop is just the first step in building a vast Hamster ecosystem that extends beyond the game itself. The airdrop rewards will be based on various factors, including overall game activity, community interaction, referral quality, achievements, wallet integration, and reputation.

Hamster Kombat leverages the immense popularity of Telegram, with its 950 million users, to create a seamless and accessible gaming experience. The game is built as a Telegram mini-app, offering advantages like TON Connect for easy wallet integration, diverse monetization options, and a thriving community for developers.

Beyond the current game, Hamster Kombat aims to become a gaming publishing ecosystem, introducing the best game studios to its massive audience. This expansion into publishing will not only bring more diverse gaming experiences to players but also generate fiat revenue, ensuring the platform's long-term sustainability.

The $HMSTR token, a community-driven token launched by the Hamster Foundation, will play a central role in the Hamster ecosystem. It will power multiple products within and outside the ecosystem, creating a thriving economy for its users.

Hamster Kombat is more than just a game; it's a gateway to Web3. By offering a fun, engaging, and rewarding experience, it's paving the way for mass adoption of cryptocurrencies and blockchain technology. With its ambitious goals and innovative approach, Hamster Kombat is set to revolutionize the play-to-earn landscape.

MemeFi

MemeFi Coin is a unique cryptocurrency-based game that operates within the Telegram messaging platform. Launched in 2024, it has gained attention as a "tap-to-earn" game that promises users the opportunity to accumulate points that will eventually be converted into a cryptocurrency token called $Memefi. The core gameplay revolves around users tapping repeatedly on their screens to "attack" a virtual character called the "Boss." Each successful tap contributes to defeating this character, which then allows players to progress to higher levels and earn more points. The game presents a twist on traditional clicker games by framing the tapping action as combat against an opponent rather than simple point accumulation.

There are several methods for earning points in MemeFi Coin. The primary method is through manual tapping, but users can also earn substantial points through a referral program by inviting others to join the game. An auto tap bot provides automated tapping for limited periods each day, while the "Earn Tab" offers additional point-earning opportunities through various tasks. Users can earn up to 1 million points by sharing sponsored posts on their Telegram stories, and a "Secret Tap Combo" feature allows users to earn 1-4 million points daily by tapping specific parts of the Boss character.

Technically, the game is built as a Telegram mini-app, accessible directly within the messaging platform. It includes an in-app wallet feature for managing earned tokens. The developers plan to build the MemeFi token on the Linear Blockchain, distinguishing it from many other crypto games that use the TON blockchain. The team behind MemeFi Coin has announced that 90% of the total token supply will be allocated to the community, with no locks or vesting periods. This generous distribution model is aimed at building trust and engagement within the user base.

Several factors contribute to the perceived legitimacy of MemeFi Coin. The decision to use Linear Blockchain lends credibility to the project, while continuous improvements and the addition of features like in-app wallets suggest ongoing commitment. Collaborations with established Web3 projects like Nomis, CoffeeMeme Coin, and BluWhale further add to its legitimacy. However, the game is not without criticisms. The gameplay can be repetitive and potentially frustrating for some users, and the auto-tap bot's functionality is limited, requiring frequent manual reactivation. As with many crypto-based games, there are inherent risks and uncertainties regarding the future value and utility of the promised tokens.

Looking ahead, the game's developers are promoting a Token Generation Event (TGE) in the future, where accumulated points will be converted into $Memefi tokens. They've also hinted at additional incentives for players who achieve higher levels in the game. While MemeFi Coin shows promise and has implemented several features to engage users, potential players should approach with caution, as is advisable with any crypto-related venture. The game's long-term success will likely depend on the developers' ability to maintain user interest, deliver on their token promises, and navigate the volatile cryptocurrency market.

TapSwap

Tapswap is a new entrant in the world of cryptocurrency airdrops, specifically designed as a "tap-to-earn" game on the Telegram platform.

Initially conceived as a decentralized exchange on the Solana blockchain, the project later pivoted to the TON blockchain, aligning itself more closely with successful predecessors like Notcoin.

The core concept of Tapswap revolves around users accumulating "shares" by tapping on their screens within the Telegram bot interface. New users start with 2,500 shares and can earn up to 500 shares per tapping session, with a cooldown period between sessions. The project's token distribution strategy allocates 50% to active community members, 30% to the treasury for platform development, and the remainder to the team, advisors, and liquidity support.

Tapswap offers several methods for users to increase their share balance. Besides tapping, users can complete various tasks such as joining Telegram groups and following social media accounts. A referral system allows users to earn additional shares when their invitees actively participate. Recently, a new earning method was introduced where users can watch YouTube videos from the official Tapswap channel and note down special codes for extra shares.

The project's legitimacy remains a topic of debate. While it shows similarities to successful projects like Notcoin, there are some concerns. The development team remains anonymous, which may raise questions for some potential participants. Additionally, the project has faced criticism for repeatedly postponing its Token Generation Event (TGE), leading to growing impatience among its user base.

Despite these challenges, Tapswap has seen significant growth since its launch, suggesting a level of community interest. The project's decision to launch on the TON blockchain, confirmed by both the Tapswap team and TON, lends some credibility to its intentions.

However, potential participants should approach Tapswap with caution. The low earning rate of 500 shares per session and the necessity of upgrades for higher earnings may be discouraging for some users. The project also faces accusations of being a "copycat" version of Notcoin, which may impact its perceived originality in the crowded crypto space.

As with many crypto projects, especially those in the airdrop and play-to-earn spaces, the future of Tapswap remains uncertain. While it offers a free way to potentially accumulate crypto tokens, users should be aware of the time investment required and the inherent risks associated with new and unproven crypto projects. The repeated postponement of the TGE and growing user frustration highlight the volatile nature of such ventures.

In conclusion, while Tapswap presents an interesting opportunity for crypto enthusiasts, it's crucial for potential participants to approach it with realistic expectations. The project's evolution from Solana to TON, the addition of new earning methods, and the challenges it faces in maintaining user interest all contribute to a complex picture of a young crypto project navigating the competitive landscape of blockchain-based rewards systems.

My Thoughts on Telegram Based Play-to-Earn Games

The rise of Telegram-based tap-to-earn games marks a significant shift in the cryptocurrency landscape, blending entertainment with financial opportunities. While Hamster Kombat, MemeFi, and TapSwap are at the forefront, other contenders like Blum, Tomarket, and Gemz are also gaining traction in this space.

These platforms offer a novel approach to token acquisition, allowing users to earn cryptocurrencies through gameplay. Should these tokens secure listings on exchanges prior to the anticipated bull run, early participants could potentially reap substantial rewards from price appreciation.

For the majority, engaging in these game-based airdrops presents an accessible method to accumulate tokens. However, those with greater financial resources might opt for alternative strategies, such as staking TON or directly purchasing tokens post-listing. Regardless of one's approach, thorough research into each project is crucial before committing time or capital.

Although the Telegram tap-to-earn phenomenon is still in its infancy, its transformative potential is clear. As the ecosystem expands with new games and a growing user base, we may witness a fundamental shift in cryptocurrency engagement and acquisition methods.

It's worth noting that the cryptocurrency sphere is characterized by rapid evolution and emerging trends. Maintaining an open mind, exploring these innovative platforms, and adhering to prudent investment practices is advisable. The upcoming bull market could very well be propelled by the creative energy emanating from Telegram's play-to-earn gaming sector.

Bull Run 2024

Chapter 7

Choosing the Right Exchange

In the untamed frontier of crypto, selecting the right exchange is akin to choosing your saloon: you seek a secure, vibrant establishment that doesn't fleece you. But with hundreds of exchanges available, each boasting unique features and quirks, how do you find your ideal match?

Did You Know?

1. Global daily crypto trading volume often surpasses $100 billion, with centralized exchanges (CEXs) handling the majority. This immense liquidity is a double-edged sword, offering abundant trading opportunities but also potential for market manipulation.
2. Despite security advancements, crypto exchanges remain prime targets for hackers.

In 2023 alone, over $3 billion worth of crypto was lost due to exchange hacks and exploits. This sobering statistic underscores the importance of choosing a secure and reputable platform.

3. The regulatory environment for crypto exchanges varies widely globally. Some nations have embraced crypto enthusiastically, while others have imposed strict regulations or outright bans. As a trader, understanding your jurisdiction's regulatory landscape is crucial.

These facts aren't mere trivia; they're vital considerations when choosing your trading arena. Let's elucidate.

Centralized vs. Decentralized Exchanges (CEXs vs. DEXs)

CEXs: Centralized exchanges like Binance, Coinbase, and Kraken are the most popular crypto trading platforms. They act as intermediaries between buyers and sellers, offering user-friendly interfaces, high liquidity, and features like margin trading and staking. CEXs typically hold custody of your assets, making them convenient for beginners but potentially vulnerable to hacks or mismanagement. They employ order book systems, listing buy and sell orders by price. The exchange's matching engine pairs buyers and sellers based on optimal executable prices for the desired quantity, determining asset prices through supply and demand dynamics relative to other currencies or cryptocurrencies.

CEXs curate available digital assets, offering some assurance against dubious cryptocurrencies.

Advantages of CEXs:

1. CEXs provide novice investors with a familiar, accessible method of trading cryptocurrencies. Unlike complex crypto wallets and peer-to-peer transactions, CEX users can easily manage their accounts and conduct transactions through apps and websites.
2. CEXs offer additional security and dependability for transactions and trading. By facilitating transactions through

established, centralized platforms, these exchanges provide increased peace of mind.
3. Some CEXs allow investors to amplify their investments using borrowed funds, known as margin trading. This can lead to higher returns, but losses may also be magnified.

Disadvantages of CEXs:

1. CEXs are operated by companies responsible for customer holdings. Large exchanges often hold substantial amounts of bitcoin, making them attractive targets for hackers and theft. The Mt.Gox incident, where the once-largest cryptocurrency exchange reported the theft of 850,000 bitcoins, leading to its downfall, serves as a cautionary tale.
2. Unlike peer-to-peer transactions, CEXs often impose significant transaction fees for their services and convenience, which can be particularly high for large-scale trading.
3. Most importantly, many CEXs act as custodians for digital assets, storing them in their own wallets rather than allowing users to maintain private keys. While convenient

for trading, this practice carries risks, including exchange failure and fraud. Recent examples include the collapse of the TerraUSD stablecoin and Luna token, bankruptcies of Three Arrows Capital, Celsius Network, Voyager Digital, and the sudden downfall of FTX and Alameda Research.

DEXs: The Wild Frontier: Decentralized exchanges like Uniswap, SushiSwap, and PancakeSwap operate on blockchain technology, eliminating intermediaries. These exchanges utilize smart contracts – self-executing blockchain code. Smart contracts offer enhanced privacy and reduced transaction costs compared to CEXs. However, the absence of an intermediary means users must be self-reliant, making DEXs more suitable for experienced investors.

Advantages of DEXs:

1. DEX users retain control of their assets without transferring them to third parties. This eliminates the risk of company hacks

and provides greater protection against failure, fraud, or theft.
2. The peer-to-peer nature of DEXs helps prevent market manipulation, safeguarding users from fraudulent trading practices.
3. DEXs don't require know-your-customer (KYC) forms, offering user privacy and anonymity. Their lack of censorship means a wider variety of cryptocurrencies and digital assets are available compared to CEXs. In fact, many Altcoins are exclusively traded on DEXs.

Disadvantages of DEXs:

1. DEX users must securely store their wallet keys and passwords, as lost assets cannot be recovered. They require users to familiarize themselves with the platform and process, unlike the more user-friendly CEXs.
2. DEXs are primarily designed for exchanging digital assets and are not well-suited for fiat currency transactions. This makes them less convenient for users without existing cryptocurrency holdings.

3. With 99% of crypto transactions occurring on CEXs, DEXs often struggle with liquidity. Low trading volumes can make it difficult to find buyers and sellers.

Your choice between CEX and DEX depends on your priorities. If you value convenience and a wide range of features, a CEX might be your best bet. But if you're privacy-conscious and tech-savvy, a DEX could be a better fit.

Going through KYC

Most reputable exchanges require completion of a Know Your Customer (KYC) process before trading. This involves providing personal information like your name, address, and government-issued ID. While seemingly cumbersome, KYC is crucial for preventing fraud and money laundering.

To navigate the KYC process smoothly:

4. Be Prepared: Have your documents ready and ensure they're up-to-date.
5. Be Patient: The verification process can take time, especially during peak periods.

6. Be Honest: Providing false information can lead to account closure and even legal trouble.

Comparing Popular Exchanges

Choosing the right crypto exchange is a crucial step for any investor or trader. Let's take a closer look at some of the most popular options, each with its unique strengths and weaknesses.

Binance, the undisputed giant of the crypto exchange world, boasts an impressive trading volume, often exceeding $50 billion daily. This massive liquidity ensures smooth transactions and tight spreads. However, Binance has faced regulatory scrutiny in several jurisdictions, and its sheer size and complexity might be overwhelming for beginners. The platform offers a tiered fee structure, with maker/taker fees starting at 0.10% / 0.10% and decreasing with higher trading volume or BNB (Binance Coin) holdings.

Coinbase, a publicly traded company known for its user-friendly interface, is a popular choice for beginners. Its educational resources, like the

Coinbase Earn program, make it easy for newcomers to learn about crypto. However, Coinbase's fees are relatively high compared to other exchanges, with spreads often exceeding 1% on some trades.

Kraken, a veteran exchange with a strong reputation for security, caters to both retail and institutional investors. It offers a wide range of trading pairs, margin trading, and staking services. Kraken's fees are competitive, with maker/taker fees starting at 0.16% / 0.26% and decreasing with higher trading volume.

Bitget, a rising star in the crypto exchange arena, is making waves with its innovative approach to security and transparency. It stands out for its monthly Merkle-based reserve audits, providing an unprecedented level of transparency around its asset backing. The exchange also employs multi-party computation (MPC) key management, CCSS Level 3 certified cold wallet storage, and robust fraud prevention systems. Bitget's trading fees are among the lowest in the industry, with spot fees as low as 0.02% for makers and 0.06% for takers. It also offers a range of advanced features like copy trading and futures grid trading, making it an attractive option for both beginners and experienced traders.

OKX, formerly known as OKEx, is a comprehensive platform offering spot trading, margin trading, derivatives, and DeFi services. It boasts a wide range of trading pairs and high liquidity. OKX's fees are competitive, with maker/taker fees typically ranging from 0.02% to 0.10% depending on the trading volume and token used for payment.

Bybit, a popular choice for derivatives traders, offers perpetual contracts with up to 100x leverage. Its user-friendly interface and copy trading feature make it accessible to both novice and experienced traders. Bybit's fees are also very competitive, with maker rebates and taker fees starting at 0.025%.

Bittrex, known for its extensive selection of altcoins, focuses on security and compliance. It offers a variety of trading pairs, though its liquidity might not be as high as some other exchanges. Bittrex's fees are generally moderate, with maker/taker fees starting at 0.75%.

Gemini, a regulated exchange based in the US, prioritizes security and compliance. It offers a limited selection of cryptocurrencies but provides a high level of trust and institutional-grade features. Gemini's fees are on the higher side, with a convenience fee and transaction fee structure that varies depending on the order size and payment method.

Each of these exchanges offers a unique value proposition, catering to different types of traders and investors. Choose your platform wisely, considering your individual needs and preferences. Remember, the best exchange for you is the one that best aligns with your trading goals, risk tolerance, and desired features.

Bull Run 2024

Chapter 8

Wallet Security

You've meticulously built your crypto portfolio, researched promising projects, and executed some shrewd trades. But where are you storing these valuable digital assets? Keeping them on an exchange is akin to leaving cash in a bustling marketplace – convenient, yet perilous. To truly possess your crypto, a secure wallet is essential.

Did You Know?

- A 2023 Glassnode study revealed that only 14% of Bitcoin holders genuinely control their private keys. This implies that the vast majority rely on third parties like exchanges to safeguard their assets.
- In 2023, over $2 billion worth of crypto was lost due to wallet hacks and exploits. This alarming statistic underscores the critical importance of proper wallet security.

- Unlike traditional banking, crypto transactions are irreversible. If you send crypto to an incorrect address or lose your private keys, there's no customer service to rectify the mistake.

These facts aren't intended to instill fear, but to empower you. By comprehending the risks and implementing necessary precautions, you can ensure the safety of your crypto assets.

Hot Wallets vs. Cold Wallets

Consider hot wallets as your everyday wallet, suitable for carrying small amounts for daily transactions. Cold wallets, conversely, are like a home safe, designed for storing larger amounts of valuables for long-term security.

Hot Wallets:

Hot wallets maintain an internet connection, offering easy access for frequent trading and transactions. They come in various forms, including mobile apps, desktop software, and web-based wallets. While convenient, they're more susceptible to hacking attempts.

Cold Wallets:

A cold wallet, also known as a hardware wallet, is a physical device designed to securely store your cryptocurrency private keys offline. This offline storage method significantly reduces the risk of online hacking attempts, making cold wallets one of the safest options for long-term cryptocurrency storage.

How Cold Wallets Work:

Cold wallets store your private keys - the cryptographic codes required to access and transfer your cryptocurrency - on a dedicated hardware device. These devices are not connected to the internet when not in use, hence the term "cold storage." To access your funds, you need to connect the device to a computer or smartphone and use the wallet's associated software.

Setting Up and Using a Cold Wallet:

1. Purchase a reputable cold wallet: Popular brands include Ledger, Trezor, and KeepKey.

2. Install the wallet's software: Download and install the official wallet software on your computer or smartphone.

3. Initialize the device: Follow the manufacturer's instructions to set up your device. This typically involves creating a PIN code for device access.

4. Generate and securely store your seed phrase: The wallet will generate a seed phrase (usually 12-24 words) that can recover your wallet if lost or damaged. Write this down and store it securely offline in multiple locations.

5. Connect the device: Use the provided USB cable or Bluetooth connection to link your cold wallet to your computer or smartphone.

6. Add cryptocurrency: Use the wallet's software to generate receiving addresses for your desired cryptocurrencies. Send funds to these addresses from exchanges or other wallets.

7. Making transactions: When you want to send cryptocurrency, connect your device, open the wallet software, and confirm the transaction on the physical device itself.

8. Disconnect and store safely: After use, disconnect your cold wallet and store it in a secure location, such as a safe.

Security Considerations:

- Never share your PIN or seed phrase with anyone.
- Regularly update the wallet's firmware to patch any security vulnerabilities.
- Consider using a passphrase in addition to your PIN for extra security.

- Be cautious of phishing attempts; only download wallet software from official sources.

While cold wallets offer excellent security, they do have some drawbacks:

- They're not free; prices typically range from $50 to $200.
- They're less convenient for frequent trading due to the need to physically connect the device.
- If you lose both your device and seed phrase, your funds may be irrecoverable.

Despite these minor inconveniences, cold wallets remain one of the most secure methods for storing significant amounts of cryptocurrency, especially for long-term holders prioritizing security over convenience.

Your choice of wallet depends on your crypto holdings and usage frequency. A prudent approach is to use a hot wallet for smaller amounts needed for regular transactions and a cold wallet for storing the bulk of your assets.

Safeguarding Your Private Keys

Private keys are the secret codes granting access to your crypto assets. Losing them is tantamount to losing the keys to your kingdom. Here are some tips for safeguarding your private keys:

- Never Share Your Keys: Don't disclose your private keys to anyone, even if they claim to represent a reputable company or exchange.
- Use Strong Passphrases: When setting up a wallet, choose a robust passphrase that's difficult to guess. Avoid using personal information or common words.
- Enable Two-Factor Authentication (2FA): 2FA adds an extra layer of security by requiring a code from your phone or another device to access your wallet.
- Backup Your Keys: Store multiple copies of your private keys in secure offline locations, such as a fireproof safe or a safety deposit box.
- Beware of Phishing Scams: Phishing attacks are a common threat in the cryptocurrency world, often targeting cold wallet users.

These scams attempt to trick you into revealing your private keys or seed phrase. Here's how to recognize and avoid them:

1. Scrutinize email addresses: Phishers often use addresses that appear legitimate at first glance. For example, instead of "support@ledger.com", you might see "support@ledger.co" or "support@1edger.com" (using a number '1' instead of the letter 'l'). Always double-check the sender's email address for subtle misspellings or additional characters.

2. Examine URLs carefully: Phishing websites may use URLs that look similar to the official one. For instance, "ledger-live.com" instead of "ledger.com". Look for extra hyphens, misspellings, or additional words in the domain name.

3. Be wary of urgent requests: Phishing emails often create a false sense of urgency, claiming your account will be closed or your funds are at risk if you don't act

immediately. Legitimate companies rarely use such tactics.

4. Check for poor grammar or formatting: Many phishing attempts contain obvious spelling errors or unusual formatting, which can be a red flag.

5. Hover over links before clicking: This will show you the actual URL the link leads to. If it doesn't match the expected official website, it's likely a phishing attempt.

6. Use bookmarks: Instead of clicking links in emails, use bookmarked links to access your wallet provider's official website.

7. Verify through official channels: If you're unsure about a message, contact your wallet provider directly through their official website or support channels.

Bull Run 2024

Social media can be a double-edged sword in the crypto world. While it's a great source for real-time information and community insights, it's also rife with misinformation and manipulation. Be cautious of pump-and-dump schemes, where influencers artificially inflate the price of a coin before selling their holdings. Always cross-reference information from social media with other sources.

FUD (Fear, Uncertainty, Doubt) is a common tactic used to manipulate market sentiment. It often involves spreading negative, and sometimes false, information about a cryptocurrency or project. Learning to recognize FUD and distinguish it from legitimate concerns is a valuable skill. Look for the source of the information, consider the motivations behind it, and always seek out multiple perspectives before drawing conclusions.

On the flip side, be equally wary of overly positive hype or "FOMO" (Fear of Missing Out) marketing. Just as negative sentiment can be manipulated, so can positive sentiment. Always approach enthusiastic claims with a healthy dose of skepticism and do your own research.

Reliable News Sources

- **Global:**
  - **Bloomberg:** A leading global business and financial news source with extensive coverage of crypto markets and regulations.
  - **Reuters:** A trusted international news agency that reports on crypto developments worldwide.
  - **The Wall Street Journal:** Provides in-depth analysis and reporting on crypto markets, regulations, and trends.
  - **Financial Times:** Offers a global perspective on crypto news and financial markets.
- **American:**
  - **Coindesk:** A leading source for crypto news, analysis, and educational content.
  - **Cointelegraph:** Provides comprehensive coverage of crypto news, market analysis, and emerging trends.

- **Decrypt:** Offers a mix of news, opinion pieces, and investigative reporting on the crypto industry.
- **The Block:** Delivers in-depth research and analysis on crypto markets, regulations, and technology.

Social Media Handles to Follow

1. **Thought Leaders:**
   - **Vitalik Buterin:** Co-founder of Ethereum, a leading voice in the crypto community.
   - **Changpeng Zhao (CZ):** CEO of Binance, the world's largest crypto exchange.
   - **Michael Saylor:** CEO of MicroStrategy, a major corporate Bitcoin holder.
   - **Anthony Pompliano (Pomp):** Crypto entrepreneur and investor, known for his bullish views on Bitcoin.
2. **Industry Analysts:**

- **Willy Woo:** On-chain analyst, provides insights into Bitcoin market cycles.
- **PlanB:** Creator of the Stock-to-Flow model for predicting Bitcoin price movements.
- **Lark Davis:** Crypto investor and YouTuber, shares market analysis and investment tips.

Online Communities

- **Reddit:**
  - **r/CryptoCurrency:** A general forum for crypto discussions, news, and memes.
  - **r/Bitcoin:** Dedicated to Bitcoin news, analysis, and community discussions.
  - **r/ethereum:** Focused on Ethereum and its ecosystem.
  - **r/defi:** Discusses decentralized finance projects and trends.
- **Twitter:** The crypto community is highly active on Twitter. Follow hashtags like

#crypto, #bitcoin, #DeFi, and #NFT to stay updated.

- **Discord and Telegram:** Many crypto projects have dedicated Discord and Telegram groups for community discussions and support.

Mastering DYOR: Your Crypto Research Arsenal

- **Project Websites and Whitepapers:** Start with the official sources. A project's website and whitepaper should provide a clear overview of its goals, technology, team, and roadmap.
- **Blockchain Explorers:** Explore blockchains like Etherscan (Ethereum) or BSCScan (Binance Smart Chain) to view transaction details, smart contracts, and other on-chain data.
- **Data Aggregators:** Platforms like CoinGecko and CoinMarketCap offer comprehensive data on crypto prices, market capitalization, trading volume, and historical charts.

- **Community Forums and Social Media:** Engage with the community on platforms like Reddit, Twitter, Telegram, and Discord to gather insights and opinions.
- **Independent Research and Analysis Platforms:** Messari, Delphi Digital, and Glassnode offer in-depth research reports, data analysis, and market insights.

Identifying and Avoiding Scams, FUD, and Misinformation

1. **DYOR (Do Your Own Research):** Never invest in a project you haven't thoroughly researched.
2. **Verify Information:** Cross-check information from multiple sources before acting on it.
3. **Beware of Emotional Appeals:** Scammers often use FOMO (Fear of Missing Out) or FUD to manipulate investors. Stay calm and rational.
4. **Don't Click on Suspicious Links:** Avoid clicking on links in unsolicited emails or messages.

5. **Use Strong Passwords and 2FA:** Protect your accounts with strong passwords and two-factor authentication.
6. **Be Skeptical of "Guaranteed Returns":** If it sounds too good to be true, it probably is.
7. **Consult Reputable Sources:** Rely on trusted news outlets, industry experts, and official project channels for information.

Bull Run 2024

Chapter 10

The Emotional Rollercoaster

The crypto landscape in 2017 was a whirlwind of exhilaration. Bitcoin's value skyrocketed, alternative coins surged, and social media overflowed with luxury car memes. Like many, I was swept up in the frenzy. Fear of missing out consumed me as I watched acquaintances seemingly amass fortunes overnight. I impulsively chased price pumps, overlooked warning signs, and made rash decisions driven by avarice.

The inevitable market collapse arrived, and my portfolio plummeted. Panic engulfed me. I liquidated everything at a loss, convinced that cryptocurrency was a fraud. However, as the turmoil subsided, I realized my gravest error wasn't investing in crypto; it was allowing my emotions to govern my choices.

I pledged to learn from my mistakes and cultivate a disciplined, long-term strategy. I immersed myself in studying market cycles, technical analysis, and risk management. I learned to harness my emotions, resist FOMO, and refrain from panic selling. Most crucially, I embraced a mindset of patience and resilience.

The 2020 bull market saw my portfolio recover and expand beyond my wildest expectations. The key to my success? It wasn't merely knowledge and strategy; it was mastering my emotions.

The Psychology of Investing

The cryptocurrency market is an emotional rollercoaster. FOMO, greed, panic, euphoria – these are just a few of the psychological forces that can wreak havoc on your portfolio if left unchecked.

FOMO (Fear of Missing Out): The sensation that you're missing a lucrative opportunity can lead to impulsive purchasing decisions.

Greed: The desire for rapid wealth can cloud judgment and result in risky investments.

Panic Selling: The fear of financial loss can cause you to sell at the most inopportune moment.

Euphoria: The excitement of gains can lead to overconfidence and reckless trading.

These emotional biases are innate to our psychology, but they can be managed with self-awareness and discipline.

Strategies for Emotional Mastery

Have a Plan: Develop a clear investment strategy with specific objectives and risk tolerance. Adhere to your plan, even amid emotional turbulence.

Set Stop-Loss Orders: These orders automatically sell your assets if the price falls below a certain threshold, shielding you from significant losses.

Take Profits: Avoid excessive greed. Establish profit targets and secure some gains when you reach them.

Diversify Your Portfolio: Don't concentrate all your investments in one area. Diversification can help mitigate risk and alleviate emotional stress.

Don't Check Your Portfolio Too Often: Obsessive monitoring can lead to emotional decisions. Establish a schedule for reviewing your portfolio, and stick to it.

Take Breaks: If you find yourself becoming emotional, step away from the market. Take a walk, listen to music, or engage in activities to clear your mind.

Seek Support: Consult a trusted friend, family member, or financial advisor if you're struggling with emotional trading.

Cryptocurrency is a long-term endeavor. Don't be discouraged by short-term volatility. Focus on your long-term objectives, and remember that patience and discipline are crucial to success in this market.

By mastering your emotions and adopting a long-term perspective, you can tame the Crypto Kraken and navigate the volatile waters with confidence. Remember, the most successful investors are not those who make the most impulsive trades, but those who remain calm, rational, and disciplined.

Conclusion

The recent downturn in late July and early August 2024 may have rattled the cryptocurrency market, but it also highlights the critical importance of risk management and adopting a long-term outlook. Those who endured this tumultuous period have gained priceless insights, while those who faltered now have a chance to bounce back stronger and more knowledgeable. As we gaze into the future, let's summarize the essential lessons from our crypto journey.

Grasping the core principles of blockchain technology and Bitcoin's historical context is essential for successfully navigating the cryptocurrency ecosystem. This foundational knowledge provides a framework for interpreting current developments and anticipating potential future trends. Selecting appropriate cryptocurrencies for investment demands thorough investigation and careful consideration. When making investment choices, evaluate factors such as technological innovation, team expertise, practical applications, and community support.

In the highly volatile cryptocurrency market, risk management is of utmost importance. Employing strategies like diversification, dollar-cost averaging, and implementing stop-loss orders are crucial techniques for safeguarding your capital and mitigating risk. Constructing a well-balanced crypto portfolio that aligns with your risk tolerance and financial objectives is vital for withstanding market turbulence and optimizing potential returns.

Venture beyond Bitcoin to explore the exciting advancements in decentralized finance (DeFi), non-fungible tokens (NFTs), and the metaverse. These emerging trends could play a pivotal role in driving the next bull run, presenting fresh investment prospects and avenues for innovation. Selecting an appropriate cryptocurrency exchange is fundamental to your trading success. When choosing your platform, consider key aspects such as security measures, fee structures, liquidity levels, and overall user experience. You must Learn before you ever dream of Earning.

Glossary of Crypto Terms

ATH (All-time high): The highest price a cryptocurrency has ever reached.

Alternative Coins (Altcoins): Any cryptocurrency other than Bitcoin.

Airdrop: The distribution of a cryptocurrency token or coin, typically for free, to numerous wallet addresses as a way of marketing a new virtual currency.

Bitcoin Maximalist: Someone who believes Bitcoin is the only cryptocurrency worth investing in.

Bitcoin to the moon: An expression used to express the belief that the price of Bitcoin will rise significantly.

Block reward: The reward given to a miner for successfully mining a block of transactions.

Blockchain: A decentralized, distributed ledger that records transactions across a network of computers.

Burn: The process of permanently removing a certain amount of cryptocurrency from circulation by sending it to an unrecoverable address, effectively reducing the supply.

CEX – Centralized Crypto Exchange: A cryptocurrency exchange that is operated by a company or organization.

Circulating Supply: The amount of a cryptocurrency that is currently in circulation and available for trading or use.

DAO: Decentralized Autonomous Organization, an organization that is run by code and governed by its members.

dApps: Decentralized applications, applications that are built on a blockchain.

DEX: Decentralized exchange, a cryptocurrency exchange that is not operated by a company or organization.

DeFi: Decentralized finance, a financial system that is built on blockchain technology.

Digital Address: A unique string of characters that identifies a particular wallet on a blockchain.

Digital Wallet: A software program or hardware device that stores your cryptocurrency private keys.

FIAT: Government-issued currency that is not backed by a commodity such as gold.

FOMO: Fear of missing out, the feeling that you are missing out on a profitable opportunity.

FUD: Fear, uncertainty, and doubt, a strategy used to spread negative information about a cryptocurrency.

HODL: A misspelling of "hold" that has become a popular term in the crypto community, meaning to hold onto your cryptocurrencies for the long term.

Halving: An event that occurs approximately every four years in which the block reward for mining Bitcoin is cut in half.

ICO: Initial Coin Offering, a fundraising method used by new cryptocurrency projects.

IEO: Initial Exchange Offering, a fundraising method similar to an ICO, but conducted on a cryptocurrency exchange.

KYC: Know Your Customer, a process used by financial institutions to verify the identity of their customers.

Liquidate: In the crypto market, liquidation occurs when a trader's position is automatically closed out by the exchange due to insufficient funds to cover losses or maintain margin requirements.

Liquidity: The degree to which an asset or security can be quickly bought or sold in the market without affecting the asset's price. In the crypto market, liquidity refers to how easily a cryptocurrency can be traded for another asset, such as fiat currency or another cryptocurrency.

Market Cap: The total value of all coins of a particular cryptocurrency that have been mined.

Mint: The process of creating new tokens or coins on a blockchain, typically associated with NFTs or new cryptocurrencies.

Mining and Miners: The process of verifying and adding transactions to the blockchain. Miners are the people or organizations that perform this work.

Portfolio Tracker: A tool or application that helps crypto investors track the value of their portfolio and monitor its performance over time.

Proof-of-stake (PoS): A consensus mechanism used by some blockchains to validate transactions and create new blocks.

Proof-of-work (PoW): A consensus mechanism used by some blockchains to validate transactions and create new blocks.

Private Key (Seed): A secret code that gives you access to your cryptocurrency wallet.

Pump & Dump: A type of market manipulation in which a group of people artificially inflate the price of a cryptocurrency and then sell it at a profit.

Satoshi: The smallest unit of Bitcoin, named after Satoshi Nakamoto, the pseudonymous creator of Bitcoin.

Shitcoin: A derogatory term for a cryptocurrency that is considered to be of little or no value.

Total Market Cap: The total value of all cryptocurrencies that have been mined.

Whale: An individual or entity that holds a large amount of a particular cryptocurrency.

Whitepaper: A document that outlines the goals, technology, and roadmap of a cryptocurrency project.

About the Author

Frederick Strong is a seasoned cryptocurrency expert, investor, and visionary known for his astute market analysis and forward-thinking strategies. With over a decade of experience in the blockchain and digital asset space, Strong has established himself as a trusted voice in the crypto community.

As the author of this book, Strong combines his deep understanding of market cycles with practical insights to help both newcomers and experienced investors navigate the complexities of cryptocurrency investing.

Strong's journey in crypto began in the early days of Bitcoin, and he has since witnessed and participated in multiple market cycles. His unique perspective comes from hands-on experience as a trader, educator, and consultant for various blockchain projects.

A frequent speaker at international crypto conferences and a regular contributor to leading financial publications, Strong is passionate about demystifying cryptocurrency and blockchain technology for the masses. His writing style blends technical analysis with accessible explanations, making complex concepts understandable to readers of all backgrounds.

When not immersed in the world of cryptocurrencies, Frederick enjoys mountain biking, practicing mindfulness, and mentoring aspiring crypto entrepreneurs. He believes that the upcoming bull run will be a pivotal moment in the history of finance and is dedicated to helping others seize the opportunities it presents.

Through "BULL RUN 2024," Frederick Strong aims to empower readers with the knowledge and confidence to make informed decisions in the exciting and often unpredictable world of cryptocurrency investing.

www.ingramcontent.com/pod-product-compliance
Lightning Source LLC
Chambersburg PA
CBHW052300220526
45471CB00001B/426